Under the Ice

Written by Jenny Feely

Flying Start
to Literacy®

Contents

Prologue

The explorer Sir Hubert Wilkins took an expedition to the Arctic in 1931. During this expedition, Wilkins and his scientists collected important new information.

This information was so accurate that it helped to save a US submarine in 1958. This submarine, the USS Skate, was patrolling the Arctic ice when its compasses stopped working. The captain of the submarine used information from Wilkins's expedition to work out the location of the submarine, saving it from disaster.

The USS Skate in the Arctic

Chapter 1

An exciting mission

On June 4, 1931, a submarine called the Nautilus left the United States. Its mission was to cross the Arctic Ocean under the ice to the North Pole.

Sir Hubert Wilkins

The Nautilus submarine was christened in New York City.

No one had ever tried to go under the Arctic ice in a submarine. Many people said that it was impossible. But the captain of the Nautilus – Sir Hubert Wilkins – was certain that it could be done.

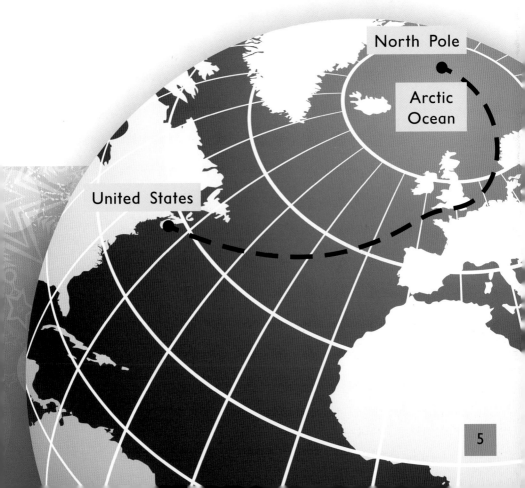

North Pole

Arctic Ocean

United States

Chapter 2

Many challenges to overcome

Exploring the Arctic in 1931 was very dangerous. The sea ice was always moving and no one knew how far down into the water it reached and whether there was land underneath or just ocean.

There were only a few months each year when such an exploration could be attempted, because it was only during the summer that breaks in the sea ice existed. Wilkins needed these breaks so the submarine could come to the surface. As winter approached, the patches of open water would freeze and disappear.

Icebergs can be dangerous for submarines because they can extend a long way down underneath the water.

shortwave radio

The only contact the Nautilus had with the outside world was through shortwave radio, and it was not certain that this would work properly through the ice. To find their way under the ice, Wilkins and his crew would need to rely on a compass. But being so close to the magnetic North Pole caused compasses to become unreliable.

compass

The Nautilus could submerge to depths of about 60 metres, but going deeper was very risky as the water pressure could squeeze the submarine until it collapsed. If the sea ice went deeper than 60 metres, it would be very difficult to navigate around it.

When underwater, the Nautilus was powered by batteries. It had to surface for eight out of every 24 hours to refresh the air supply and to run the diesel engines, which recharged the submarine's batteries. To do this, the crew had to find breaks in the sea ice.

As this could be difficult, Wilkins had the Nautilus fitted with an ice drill, which could drill through the ice so that the Nautilus could reach the surface. But no one knew for sure if this would work.

breaks in the Arctic ice

Chapter 3

A shaky start

For the expedition, Wilkins leased a submarine from the US Navy and called it Nautilus. This submarine had never been to the Arctic and had to be remodelled to make it suitable. It took many months and, before it was even finished, the project was running late.

When the submarine was ready, it had to be tested. Filled with all of the equipment needed to explore the Arctic, the Nautilus was heavier than expected, and it plummeted downwards, finally getting stuck in the mud 80 metres below the surface.

The Nautilus is being prepared for its expedition.

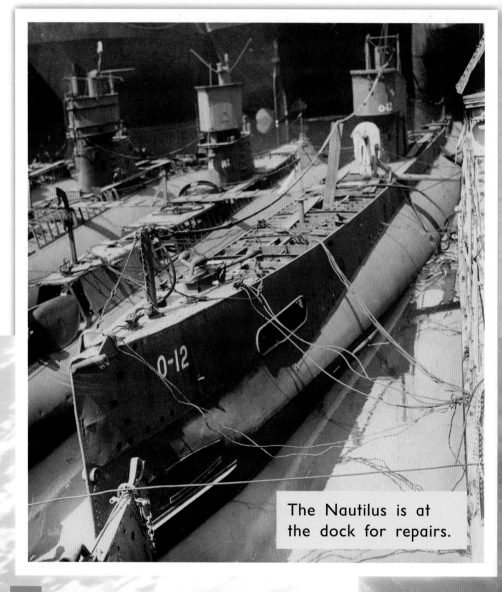

The Nautilus is at the dock for repairs.

The Nautilus was in danger of being crushed by the pressure of the water. The captain and crew tried everything to free the Nautilus from the ocean floor – using engines, emptying the ballast tanks that weighed it down, even having the crew run from side to side to try to rock the submarine out of the mud. Nothing seemed to work. Then suddenly, without any explanation, the Nautilus began to rise to the surface. Disaster had been avoided – this time.

Explorer facts

Wilkins named the submarine after the submarine Nautilus in the book *Twenty Thousand Leagues Under the Sea* by Jules Verne.

After more tests, and now two months behind schedule, the Nautilus set off across the surface of the ocean for Norway. This was where Wilkins planned to launch his expedition. But after only three days at sea, they sailed into a frightening storm.

The Nautilus sails through stormy seas.

The Nautilus bucked and rolled as the huge waves tossed it around. All the members of the crew became seasick. Water seeped into one of the submarine's engines and it stopped working. Soon the second engine failed as well.

A crew member checks machinery on the submarine.

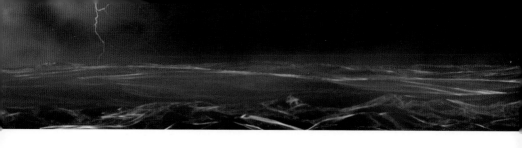

For three days the storm raged. The crew needed to send for help, but there was not enough power left to run the radio. The radio operator worked on the radio, changing it so that it could send out a low whistling sound using the small amount of power left. For 18 hours he tapped out a message in Morse code: SOS, SOS, SOS.

Eventually the Nautilus was rescued by a US navy ship and was towed to safety.

Explorer facts

SOS is the traditional message used in emergencies and it means help is needed. It stands for Save Our Souls.

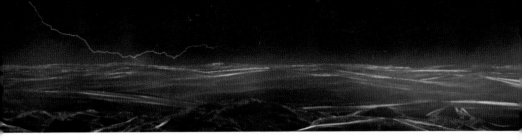

The Nautilus was taken to a dock in England to be repaired.

Chapter 4

Into the unknown

The Nautilus needed many repairs. These took one month and set the expedition even further behind schedule.

At last the Nautilus was ready and set off for the Arctic ice. After battling another vicious storm, the submarine reached the Arctic ice.

The crew celebrated stepping onto the Arctic ice for the first time.

When Wilkins ordered the crew to prepare for the first dive under the ice, they discovered that the diving rudders were missing. These were vital because they were used to steer the submarine when it was underwater.

No one knew if they had been lost in the storm or if a crew member, frightened of going under the ice, had tried to ruin the expedition on purpose.

But Wilkins was determined that the expedition would not be a total failure. Although it was impossible to cross the Arctic Ocean under the ice, he ordered that the scientists collect as much scientific information as they could.

Scientists set up their equipment on the Arctic ice.

The scientists began to collect data about the depth of the Arctic Ocean floor, the flow of the ocean water and the direction in which it moved, and the level of salt in the water. They took samples of the mud on the ocean floor and made observations of the animal life. This was the first time such data had ever been collected.

A scientist collects information.

Chapter 5

One final attempt

Summer was nearly over and the ice was getting thicker – time was running out for the expedition. But Wilkins was still determined to succeed. When the weather was clear, he gave the order to dive under the ice. This was very brave and perhaps very foolish – without the diving rudders, no one knew if the submarine could get back to the surface.

As the Nautilus moved slowly forward, a loud, terrifying noise reverberated through the submarine. The top of the submarine was scraping along the underside of the ice. The crew checked the inside of the submarine, but they found no damage. So the Nautilus continued on.

The Nautilus sails through ice before diving.

As the submarine floated under the ice, Wilkins and the crew saw the jagged shapes of the bottom of the ice – a sight that had never been seen by humans before. They were astounded by the colours and shapes, as the clouds moved above the ice and the sunlight shone through.

A view from under the ice.

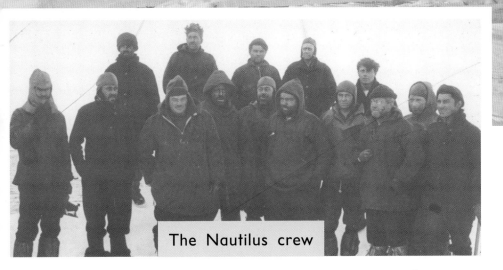

The Nautilus crew

When it was time to come out from under the ice and go back to the surface, everyone on the submarine waited nervously. The captain set the engines for slow and the Nautilus slowly glided forward, out from under the ice and into the sunshine.

Wilkins and his crew had succeeded! They were the first people to travel under the Arctic ice in a submarine.

Explorer facts

In 1958 the USS Nautilus (named after Wilkins's submarine) made the first crossing of the Arctic Ocean under the ice.

Timeline: 1931

June 4
The Nautilus departs New York and is damaged by a storm.

June 15
The Nautilus is rescued and towed to England for repairs.

New York

gust 31

Nautilus dives
er the ice.

August 23

The Nautilus reaches Arctic waters,
965 kilometres from the North Pole.

otember 20

Nautilus returns
pitsbergen; all
crew survive.

August 11

The Nautilus arrives
at the island of
Spitsbergen, Norway.

Norway

August 5

The Nautilus leaves
Bergen, Norway.

England

July 28

The Nautilus is repaired
and leaves England.

A note from the author

As a writer I find that the very best, most compelling stories are those about real people and the astonishing things they have done. When I read the biography of Sir Hubert Wilkins, I found a wealth of amazing stories.

I was especially interested in his submarine voyage under the Arctic ice. I had not realised how difficult such a voyage would be or that submarines were so dangerous and isolated. But mostly I was impressed by the ways that Wilkins persisted in terrible circumstances, not giving up when most people would.